Hello!

Thank you for buying my book!

When I was twenty-three, I had a breakdown and entered therapy. On my first day, I told my therapist that I only knew two things about myself: I was a blonde and liked pizza. That was it. Blonde and pizza.

I didn't know what I liked, thought, enjoyed, wanted, or did well. I had no moral code or opinions. My self-esteem came from how people treated me. I had severe impostor syndrome, an inner negative voice that talked non-stop, and anxiety through the roof. I was co-dependent and severely depressed.

A big part of my healing process was uncovering the childhood rules that controlled my life and then giving myself permission to write new rules.

This book is a collection of those new rules which set me free to enjoy a life filled with joy and peace.

They may not all resonate with you, but maybe you'll find a few that work for you. My hope is that you'll uncover your own childhood rules that do not serve you and replace them with rules that do, so that you too can enjoy an amazing life filled with joy and peace.

With much love,

Jennifer

PERMISSION GRANTED

Live Your Life Full of Joy and Peace

JENNIFER STANDISH

Cover Design & Interior Layout by Ronda Taylor

An Imprint for GracePoint Publishing (www.GracePointPublishing.com)

MYTHIC
LITERARY

GracePoint Matrix, LLC
624 S. Cascade Ave, Suite 201
Colorado Springs, CO 80903
www.GracePointMatrix.com
Email: Admin@GracePointMatrix.com

SAN # 991-6032

A Library of Congress Control Number has been requested and is pending.

ISBN: (Paperback) 978-1-955272-66-7

Books may be purchased for educational, business, or sales promotional use.
For bulk order requests and price schedule contact:
Orders@GracePointPublishing.com

BODY

1

love your body like you would
a child, unconditionally.

As a child, I was told that nobody would love me if I was fat. I was dieting in second grade. At seventeen, I was bulimic. I didn't have a love/hate relationship with my body. It was a hate/hate relationship.

I treated my body the way my mother treated me. I only loved my thighs if they were thin.

After forty years of berating myself because I wasn't tall and slim, I became much kinder to my body. I started to look at parts of my body that I didn't like as a child. I promised them that I would love them no matter what they looked like and will always be grateful for what they do for me.

When you become critical of your body, think of it as a child and love it unconditionally.

2

feel sexy as is.

Beauty is defined by what society considers perfect dimensions and proportions.

Know this: you can be very sexy, regardless of your shape and size—if you have confidence.

When I was in therapy, I worked at a strip club on Sunset Boulevard selling sodas and juice. It was a great job because it covered my bills, gave me a lot of free time to heal, and taught me that beauty and being sexy are not the same thing.

The dancers who made the most money were not the most beautiful or the best dancers but were the most confident, which on stage translated to sexy. These women were confident in their skin, looked people in the eyes, and walked with purpose.

The next time you get naked with someone remember this: Confidence is sexy regardless of what you look like.

Hint: Red light bulbs hide a lot of flaws so make sure to switch out your regular lights. Just sayin'.

3

forgive food.

I had a terrible relationship with food for forty years. Being told that no one would love me if I was fat made food the enemy.

Food is not an enemy to be conquered. It's energy that our bodies need to function, and some of that energy is delicious.

The next time you say you hate food, please remember that you need it to survive.

4

**wear clothes that
make you feel great.**

I'm not a glamorous person. I'm a Warrior Woman. You take me into battle. I'm not someone who sits and looks pretty. I need clothes that flow over my body, giving my hips room to sway. It's what I like and that is all that matters.

I happen to find people in grungy clothes interesting. When standing in line at Home Depot, I'm always curious what projects people are working on. You can always tell the ones who are in the middle of fixing something they broke or ran out of something and had to run to the store.

Please wear clothes that make you feel good. The people who love you won't care.

5

not be thin.

That's it. Give yourself permission to not be thin.

6

embrace bedhead.

I grew up in the 90s when grunge was really big. No one washed their hair every day. We wore ripped clothes and lots of flannel. I loved it. In fact, I never evolved. I still put my wet hair up in a bun and go on with my day.

I know it's not good for your hair but I love the messiness of it. There's something that I find attractive about it. I like it on me, and I like it on other people so go ahead and rock bedhead.

7

stop dieting.

Diets are a feminist issue. HARD STOP.

People must reject the thin ideal and pressure to diet. In doing so they will get back the time, energy, and money spent pursuing unattainable ideals.

To a marketing person, chasing the unattainable is called "aspirational" messaging. It sucks the life out of us.

What could you accomplish if you simply loved your body as is?

Be healthy. Move your body. Breath deeply. Spend time in nature. Listen to music that moves you. Feed yourself what your body craves. Sleep. Be happy.

8

not wear a traditional bathing suit.

I think bathing suits are backward. Women would do better wearing men's swim trunks and a tank top because for those of us that have big thighs and a big ass, wearing a traditional bathing suit is not flattering or comfortable.

I want to be happy, and this is what makes me happy swimming.

You can do it too.

9

lie naked in the sun.

This is something that I just started doing. In the morning I get up and make coffee. I take a shower and then I go out to my deck and I lay in the sun naked.

No one can see me and I only do it for ten to fifteen minutes. But let me tell you how wonderful it feels to have the sun's warmth on every inch of my body.

The experience healed me in ways I wasn't expecting. I'm far more forgiving of my imperfections. I'm more comfortable being naked.

I suggest that you try it.

SELF-LOVE

10

go see a movie in a theater alone.

I wept the first day I went to the movies by myself. I could not have felt lonelier. For some reason, I believed I was a huge failure because I didn't have anyone to go with me.

Looking back, I don't remember why it was so traumatic for me. I must have been in an enormous amount of pain being single.

The next time you can't find anyone to go to the movies with, go alone. You'll discover how nice it is to enjoy the world solo.

11

draw as many lines in the
sand as you need.

People around you need to know your boundaries. Communicate your needs and those who love you will act accordingly.

I had a roommate who was bat-shit crazy. I didn't mind in the beginning because I just wanted her money to pay the bills. Towards the end of her lease, she went off the rails. When I tried to enforce my boundaries, she went bananas.

It is our responsibility to remove people from our lives who consider our reasonable boundaries absurd.

Go create as many boundaries as you need. There is no limit and they're free!

12

forgive, and keep the door closed.

Forgiving someone sets you free. It does not mean that you need to welcome them back into your life.

For many years I thought that if I forgave someone I would want them back in my life. That's not true. You can forgive without opening your front door to chaos.

If you have someone in your life that you are struggling to forgive, tell yourself that forgiveness and friendship are independent of one another.

13

have high standards for the people
you accept into your life.

Don't compromise your standards just to fill your life with people. Leave room for when members of your group find you. You'll be lonely for a while, but finding the right people is worth waiting for.

When I knew that my life was starting to grow in a big way, I looked around at the people I was spending most of my time with. They were good people but were incompatible with where I was going. I had to pull away.

Slowly I started to meet friends who were on the same trajectory as me.

The next time you imagine your future self, look around at the folks who support you. It's okay if you have to pull away as I did.

14

create a life that you love
before you commit to someone.

When you are truly happy, making time to date will be difficult, but that's a good thing. Your standards will go sky-high.

I will rearrange my schedule for amazing men only.

The next time you are longing for a relationship, ask yourself if you are truly happy with your life as is. If not, work on creating an amazing life before looking for a relationship. It's the easiest way to attract amazing people.

15

be a late bloomer.

It's a gift to achieve success later in life because you get to experience it with years of wisdom. Be grateful that your best life has yet to come. It's an opportunity that few get to experience.

Imagine a life where you peaked at thirty. What would you do for the rest of your life?

The next time you are frustrated that success has not found you, be grateful, and keep working at it. When it happens, you'll be more well-rounded and fulfilled as a result.

16

forgive yourself.

I was a mess for the first forty years of my life. All my decisions were based on fear. I hurt people. I hurt my career. I hurt myself. Nothing escaped my bad decisions.

In order to live a bigger and more fulfilling life, I had to forgive myself.

I told myself that I was simply ill-prepared to make good decisions. I did the best I could at the time.

The next time you start beating yourself up about something you did, stop and ask yourself if you could truly have done better given the situation?

All we can ask of ourselves is to do the best we can.

17

**not go over the bridge
until you have to.**

Don't rush into decisions because it makes you feel safe. Giving decisions breathing space allows events to unfold that, in the end, may bring about the best outcome for everyone. Stay still and wait.

I had a hard time living in limbo, so I made decisions prematurely, often to my detriment. Eventually, I learned that if I don't interfere, often situations resolved themselves for the better.

If you can wait until the dust settles to make a decision, do it. It will be hard in the beginning, but you'll get used to it.

18

not keep an immaculate home.

There are more important things to spend your energy on. Get over it. No one on their deathbed wishes that they had kept a cleaner house.

Your home is not a reflection of your value. Shit happens.

I rest a lot because, as an empath, people exhaust me easily. I also struggle with depression, which makes me tired. There are weekends when I don't get out of bed. I used to think I was lazy but the more I learned about myself I realized that staying in bed for me is selfcare.

A clean home should never trump mental wellbeing.

When you panic because someone is at the door unannounced and your house is a mess, don't do anything. They will go away, eventually.

19

stop waiting.

You are fully responsible for creating an amazing life. No one is going to do it for you. No one is going to pick you out of a crowd of people and give you a great life. It's all on you.

When I was young, I wanted someone who had an amazing life to find me so that I could piggyback off his life. Sounds great, right? But let's think that through. Would someone who has created an amazing life pick a partner who has chosen to sit back and wait for it to be handed to her? Probably not.

It took me a long time to accept responsibility for my life. It was not easy or fun for a long time, but there was no alternative.

You get out of life what you put into it.

20

not go down with the ship.

I'm tenacious and as a result, when things go south, I stay on the ship rather than jumping into a lifeboat. I simply have a hard time giving up.

I have lost a lot of time and money doing things like trying to fix an electric drill.

"The drill is not broken. It just needs new brushings at $1.99. I'll be damned if I throw this away when the fix is so simple."

Fast forward two months, I've yet to find the right part so I had to buy a new drill to see what the brushings look like so that I don't end up buying the wrong type again. I'm now waiting for another set of carbon brushings.

A new drill is $17.00. At my hourly rate, I've lost over $1,000 trying to fix the original (Eye roll). A time management consultant would have a field day with me.

I have no advice as to when to give up. Just be aware of how you spend your time.

21

break something.

Just because you don't know how to do something doesn't mean you are not magnificent. Mistakes are learning experiences.

When I start using a new tool, I break it. My first wood-turning lathe has dents all over it. My Hobie Cat sailboat is taking a beating right now. I ruined my drill press. I've gone through four chainsaws. Breaking things is my way of learning how things work. It's my process. I suck at everything new.

When working in the woodshop with my father, he often told me "Let me do that so that if I make a mistake I'm mad at myself and not you." He would have a fit if he saw my shop. It's full of projects that went south, and I love it.

The next time you break something, please don't beat yourself up about it. It may be your process too.

22

return an item that doesn't fit,
is broken, or you don't like.

This sounds crazy. Recently I almost did not return a pair of eyeglasses that had the wrong prescription because I didn't want the sales rep to think that I was fussy.

Why would I be concerned if a sales rep likes me? I shouldn't be. But for ten minutes I really tried to convince myself to just stay quiet.

The next time you purchase an item that doesn't fit, is broken, you simply don't have the need for it or you don't like it, please return it. No one will care.

23

be messy.

Women are supposed to be clean, very clean, crystal clean, clean house, clean rooms, clean clothes, clean, clean, clean. But I am not clean. If it wasn't for my Airbnb business, I would never clean my house.

I'm just messy. I'm okay with it and you can be too.

24

**make decisions that
are in your best interest.**

One day my therapist and I were talking about how people make decisions, and he was of the opinion that healthy people make decisions based on their best interest. WWHHHAATT???

This shocked me. At the time, I didn't think everybody made decisions that were in their best interest. I thought many of us looked at the people involved in the decision, the repercussions of the decision, and then decided whether or not to make it.

It's identical to putting an oxygen mask on yourself first so that you can help others put their masks on. You can't help people if you're dead.

Put yourself first. No one else will.

25

be okay that some people
may not like you.

If I were a dog, I'd be a golden retriever. When I was young, I wanted to be liked by everyone.

I wish I had been told that not everyone is going to like me and that is okay because I'm not going to like everyone either.

It's okay that you don't like everyone you meet. The world is a big place. Just find your group and move on.

26

not have a fully decorated home.

All I need is a bed. I can live in bed. I can work in bed. I watch movies in bed. I eat in bed. I can do almost anything in bed, which is why I don't have a fully decorated home that Martha Stewart would be proud of.

My furniture is actually deck furniture that I bring inside when the weather gets cold. My thinking is that if it worked as a table outside, it will work as a table inside.

If you don't want an adult home, don't have an adult home. It's your choice.

27

stay home when you are sick.

I was always pushed to go to school when I was sick. As a consequence, I didn't learn how to take care of myself. I would go to work sick when I should have stayed home a few days earlier to nip it in the bud.

Now, when I start to feel tired I put myself to bed. I don't want to get sick so I try to head it off at the pass.

The next time you think you are getting sick, stay home. You might be surprised how quickly you recover.

28

not answer the phone or
respond to an email or a
text message immediately.

You don't have to answer the phone when it rings. You also don't have to respond to an email or text immediately. In fact, the response window of time is twenty-four hours.

Most of us do not live in a world where we have to be available 24/7. Take advantage of the twenty-four hours you have to respond. Allow the situation to unfold.

Try it for a week and see how it feels.

29

spend all day in bed
without feeling guilty.

I have always been a sleeper, and along with that, I always considered myself lazy.

When I realized I was an empath, I started giving myself permission to rest.

Introverts, empaths, and highly sensitive people need to sleep to heal and recharge. It's a requirement. We get sick if we don't.

Moving forward, don't feel guilty for needing more rest than everyone else.

30

ask for help.

This is really hard for me. I never learned how to ask for and receive help. I'm so used to doing things without help that now when someone offers to help, I decline.

This must have something to do with not receiving help when I needed it. When I was bulimic, my mother told me to stop eating her food if I'm just going to throw it up. I probably needed help at that moment.

The next time you need help, ask yourself if there is someone with whom you could ask. Start with small things. You'll learn really quickly who you can rely on.

MINDSET

31

change your mind.

You have every right to change your mind. Don't let the fear of disappointing someone interfere with taking care of yourself. Your value and worth are not dependent on other people's approval.

My spirit animal is a golden retriever who says yes to every invitation. This is in direct conflict with my introverted homebody nature.

To keep my sanity, I had to learn how to tell someone that I had changed my mind. To my surprise, my friends were really cool about it.

Remember, if someone falls apart because you changed your mind, don't own it. There are many ways to react, and that person is choosing to fall apart.

32

stop being in pain.

It saddens people when I tell them that I'm not in contact with my biological family. I try to explain that while the situation is sad, it is not painful.

This is the difference. To me, sad is similar to unfortunate, it is what it is, and c'est la vie.

Pain, however, interferes with one's life. You feel pain in your body.

The next time you are in pain over a situation, ask yourself if experiencing pain is really necessary. It might not be.

33

accept responsibility for your life.

In terms of family, I got a shit deal. I would not be surprised if, when I die, God comes running over and apologizes for putting me in the wrong family.

I struggled with accepting responsibility for my life. The mantra was "if only I had a better family, I could have done something big with my life. Imagine what I could have accomplished." I said this a lot in large part because I always had a nagging feeling I was destined for something big, but I couldn't figure out what that something was.

A few years ago, after I said some version of the above, a friend of mine said, "Maybe. Maybe not."

HARD STOP.

She was right. Having a wonderful family does not necessarily mean things would have turned out better for me. We'll never know, which is why I had to move on and accept responsibility for my life. It also helped me forgive them.

What happened to you matters, but how you respond to it matters more.

34

be grateful.

Even in the worst of situations, you can find little pearls. Sometimes these little pearls are hard to see but try to find them. They can bring you joy in the worst of times.

A friend of mine inherited a beautiful farmhouse that had been in the family for generations. After living in it for ten years, it burned to the ground. She lost everything. After the shock subsided, she told me that the fire was actually a blessing in disguise. She was relieved at not having to maintain a historical structure. She also found it freeing; she could now move anywhere in the world.

The next time life seems to fall apart, pause. Slowly look around for the little pearls. They will be there, I promise.

35

not own other people's feelings.

We are in complete control over our thoughts, feelings, and behavior. How someone reacts to something is not your fault or responsibility. They are choosing to be, say, devastated. Recognize that it's their choice. They could choose something different. Don't attach your self-esteem to other people's whims and fancy.

I dated a man whose self-esteem fully depended on how well the people at work treated him. It was exhausting to come home every day because I never really knew what to expect.

Is self-esteem really self-esteem if it comes from outside yourself?

Self-esteem comes from within. The other kind is called other-esteem.

36

experiment with life choices.

When I was in my twenties and thirties, I made a ton of mistakes because I didn't know what I liked or what made me happy. I spent fifteen years experimenting with big life choices. It took so long because I had to give myself permission to:

1. *Put my needs first,*
2. *Make myself happy,*
3. *Get out of my comfort zone and try something new,*
4. *Consider the outcome as a learning opportunity,*
5. *Be okay if it doesn't work out, and then,*
6. *Execute the decision.*

Please don't be discouraged. The process gets easier with each decision. Eventually, you'll enjoy a life YOU created.

37

fall off the horse.

When I entered therapy at twenty-three, I thought that eventually I would graduate and get a diploma designating me mentally healthy. Woo hoo!

Imagine my surprise and sadness when I realized that I would never be done.

I asked myself, if self-improvement doesn't have a destination and mental health can't be measured, how am I to gauge my progress or compare my mental health to others? How was I to trust my instincts if I didn't know the degree to which I was mentally healthy?

Eventually, I realized that I will always have bad ideas and behavior. It's what I do with them that is important.

- *Do I stop and consider the repercussions?*
- *Do I give myself time to make a decision?*
- *Do I give myself permission to change my mind?*
- *Do I consider alternatives?*
- *Do I forgive myself when I make a bad decision?*
- *Do I try again?*

Asking these questions is how you know you are healing.

Please don't pressure yourself to behave perfectly all the time.

Give yourself permission to fall off the horse and be confident that you'll get back on it with grace.

38

believe that you are destined
for something big.

Deep down inside I always knew that I was destined for something great.

Regardless of where I worked, I had this nagging feeling that something wasn't right. I didn't know where to look or what to do. I simply had faith that everything would be revealed to me.

The feeling of being destined for greatness was, of course, in direct conflict with the role I was assigned in my family—I was the dumb one.

A concerted effort was made to have me believe I was dumb and wouldn't amount to anything. I was told I had brain damage. I was told I wouldn't get into college. I was told that when good things happened to me, it was because of dumb luck.

Please resist the need to be accepted by people who play small.

Play big and you'll find your people.

39

have faith that everything is going to work out just fine without evidence.

I need evidence that will stand up to scientific rigor.

When I was married and money was tight, I would have panic attacks. My poor husband didn't understand why I was worried. He would tell me "It's going to be fine." I would then ask, "How is it all going to be fine? I need details." Of course, he didn't have details, so I stayed in bed.

One day, I just stopped caring. What is the worst that could happen to me? I have a lot of money saved in retirement accounts that I could always access. What could possibly happen that I couldn't handle?

You can handle anything that comes your way. Have faith that it will work out just fine because it always has.

40

daydream.

Every successful person has spent years daydreaming about what their life will look like when they make it big.

Walking down the red carpet, receiving a Nobel Prize, standing on the top of the podium, ringing the Nasdaq bell, walking out of a bank debt-free, donating a huge amount of money to a favorite charity, and other accomplishments started as daydreams.

If you believe in the Law of Attraction, daydreaming is a way to tell the Universe what you want in incredible detail.

Allow yourself to daydream with no judgment.

41

assume responsibility for a
problem you didn't create.

I take care of a colony of feral cats. I didn't create the feral cat problem in my neighborhood but I accept responsibility for spaying or neutering and immunizing the cats that come onto my property. Even though it can be heartbreaking, I find it incredibly rewarding.

If you are in a place of great need, look around and see where you can give back. You'll be surprised at how quickly you start to receive little miracles in your own life.

42

be a proud crafter.

My basement could easily be considered a junior Michael's Craft Store. I have more supplies for projects that I had the best intentions to do but never did.

Paint, canvases, calligraphy workbooks, mosaic tiles, clay, jewelry supplies, tiny tools, lightbox, an old-fashioned paper cutter, paintbrushes, custom adult paint by number kits, fabric, wax, fragrances, paper making machine, glue, mortar, sewing machine, rope, burlap … .

My latest craze is custom adult paint by number kits. I love them because I get to paint without needing to think.

Don't be embarrassed if you're like me. Crafting reduces anxiety and stress, increases focus, and provides people with a sense of accomplishment.

43

keep a journal.

I had a fear of writing so great that when I bought my first journal I put a list of rules on the front page that included:

March 11, 1994

Journal Rules:

- *There are no misspelled words.*
- *There are no grammar or punctuation rules.*
- *Complete sentences are not a must.*
- *You don't need to know how to write to keep a journal.*

Pretty funny, right? The stress of writing in a journal was so great that I had to give myself the okay to make mistakes in my own journal that no one would read.

Even if you don't think you can write or you think you don't have anything to write about, try it. You might find, as others have, that journaling has many benefits.

44

be a crazy cat lady.

I fit the description of a crazy cat lady. I care for a colony of feral cats. I spay or neuter every feral that comes on my property. I feed and provide heated shelter. If they get sick or injured, I get them medical care.

If taking care of animals who can't survive in the wild on their own makes me a crazy lady, I'm good with that.

Don't be afraid of becoming a crazy cat lady. We have a board game, Crazy Cat Lady Game, an action figure, and National Cat Lady Day (April 19).

45

publish a typo.

OMG. To the folks who think typos mark the end of the world, please step back and realize that no one will remember it tomorrow.

Did you know that really smart people struggle with proofreading their own work? I'm not sure if that is true but it makes me feel better.

The next time you realize you made a typo, move on. Don't beat yourself up about it. "It's okay not to be perfect."

46

not finish the to-do list.

I love checking the completed box on a to-do list. I also enjoy giving myself permission to not start or finish something. I'm an adult and I get to choose how I want to spend my time and money, and so do you.

When I was in my early twenties I spent every Friday cleaning my tiny apartment. I was searching for control whereas I should have been out drinking margaritas with co-workers. I would have made more friends, more professional connections, and had a ton of fun.

Now that I'm not looking to control anything, my home is one big unfinished project, and I love it that way. There is always something fun to look at and talk about.

Your life isn't a to-do list. Stop paying attention to all the things you think you need to do and concentrate on all the things you want to do.

RELATIONSHIPS

47

stop sacrificing your needs and wants to make other people happy.

Stop staying in relationships because you don't want to hurt the other person's feelings. Breaking up with someone often means someone will get hurt.

You are not responsible for how the other person reacts and recovers. Stay in your lane and do what is in your best interest. The same is true for roommates and friends.

By trying to protect someone's feelings, you are doing yourself and them a disservice. The more you let people come and go, the more love and friendships you'll have.

48

let love go.

We hold onto things when it would be better to let things come and go.

After my marriage, I had an epiphany. If I wanted a life full of love, I should have let people come in and out of my life rather than holding on to relationships that didn't work.

I would have had more love if I created space for new people to come in.

I did the exact opposite of what I should have done. Don't be like me. Let people come and go because people will always come.

49

break up with a friend.

Just like you can leave a romantic relationship, you can leave a friendship.

Friendships can be abusive, co-dependent, one-sided, or neglectful.

I try really hard to make friendships work, but when I'm done, SLAM, I'm done. It is the last play in my playbook, and it is usually permanent.

I recommend that you take a good look at your friendship circle. Who would you be proud to bring to an awards ceremony?

50

walk away from someone who
doesn't love you the way
you need to be loved.

You are not loving someone if they can't feel it.

It's like chores. If I ask you for help, I need you to do it my way. Otherwise, you are not helping.

If you claim to love me, you need to love me the way I feel love. Otherwise, you are not loving me. You are wasting energy.

The next time you feel unloved, ask yourself if the person is loving you the way they want to love you.

If they do indeed love you but are not doing it in the right way, you need to tell them what works. And if they can't figure it out, mooooove on.

51

stop dating someone whose
family does not like you.

I used to think that problematic in-laws were not that big of a deal. Having experienced it a few times, I'm now adamant that they like me a lot.

In college, I dated someone whose mother hated me. There was nothing I could do about it. There was no fixing it. I watched my boyfriend struggle with loving his mother while wanting to protect me from her.

My husband's family wasn't crazy about me either. They lived abroad, so I thought it wouldn't affect our lives much.

For years I watched him fly home for month-long visits. Whenever he could take time off, he flew home. Not once did he ever want to go on vacation with me. It broke my heart because I never felt like I was a top priority.

If you are dating someone and don't get along with their family, leave. You'll be happier for it.

52

stop dating opposites.

Find someone exactly like yourself so that you don't live a life full of compromises. Fascinating people who can expand your horizons are better friends than partners.

I've dated men who were wildly different from me because I thought they would make interesting partners. In the beginning, they were interesting, but in the end, life was one big compromise.

I no longer want to compromise my happiness, so I'm looking for someone who is exactly like me.

The next time you are attracted to someone with whom you have nothing in common, tell yourself that it's best for them to remain a friend.

53

**stop dating people
just because they like you.**

I dated a few people because they liked me, and I felt I owed it to myself to at least get to know the person.

I wasted so much time dating lovely men who "picked me."

But life is not gym class.

When I first moved to NYC, I met a nice young man at a party. I remember thinking that I should get up and meet other people because I wasn't interested in him. Did I get up? NOPE. Should I have? YUP. But, he liked me; he liked me a lot.

I paid heavily for this mistake, and he did too. The next time you are asked out, make sure you like the person and are not just flattered.

54

put your happiness first.

When you are happy and fulfilled you have so much more to give the world. Don't put other people's happiness before your own.

When I was in college I thought that if I did what made my partner happy, they would in turn do things that made me happy. NOPE. NOPE. NOPE.

They truly didn't realize what I was doing because they would have done it with or without my participation. It made no difference to them.

Put your happiness first and you teach people what makes you happy. If they actively participate in your happiness, great. If not, you are still doing things that make you happy.

55

**not accept other people's
opinions of you.**

Everyone is entitled to their opinion, good, bad, or indifferent, but that doesn't mean their opinions are true. Your opinion is the only one that matters. Even if your opinion is bananas, it still is the only one that matters.

When you need people to love and accept you to the degree that you are willing to compromise your happiness, you become like a weeping willow always swaying on the wind. It's exhausting.

Don't give your happiness away. You are the only one who knows what is best for you.

56

apologize but don't give blood.

I admit it. As a teenager, I was not easy to be with. I was in so much pain that I just wanted to be left alone to do as I pleased. It was a horrible time to be me.

As a young adult, I felt the need to apologize to my sisters for ruining their childhoods. My therapist told me that it's okay to apologize but don't give blood. He said that I was a child too and it was never my responsibility to make my family happy.

Now whenever I feel the need to apologize, I tell myself "Don't give blood."

It's okay to take responsibility for your behavior but don't over apologize.

57

**ask for someone's
undivided attention.**

I believe that giving somebody your undivided attention is one of the greatest gifts to receive.

When you focus on someone, you're telling that person that they are really important to you and that you are setting aside everything in your life to listen to them exclusively. It's very healing.

Don't be afraid to ask for someone's undivided attention. There's nothing wrong with saying, "I need five minutes of your undivided attention to talk to you about something."

58

be happy that you are single.

It's taken me a long time to be happy that I'm single. Like many of you, I was programmed to believe that marriage equals happiness.

After years of dating and living with people, being single means I don't compromise on anything. I do as I please, always. I'm free to be me.

I recommend that people deepen their friendships and let romantic love come and go.

59

protect yourself.

When I was married, I made some pretty bad decisions about my future. I stopped saving money for retirement because my husband was younger than me and when I was going to retire he was going to be in his prime earning years. I looked at him as my retirement plan, which is really crazy.

I should have made decisions in my marriage that would have protected me should the marriage not work out. I didn't protect myself enough.

I recommend that when you're making decisions in a partnership of any kind, hold on to your power and the direction of your life.

60

push back when you don't agree.

When I was in my twenties I didn't have an opinion.

If I was asked a question I would look around the room to see what the general consensus was and go with that.

I didn't believe I was capable of defending myself should I disagree with something.

It took me a long time to realize that I didn't have to explain myself to anyone.

I can say (and you can too), "I don't agree" and not delve deep into details citing scientific research reports.

61

forgive someone who you once
thought was unforgivable.

When I got divorced I felt like the rug got pulled out from underneath me. I had no idea what had just happened and had a really hard time understanding how somebody could change their mind on so many things. I honestly didn't believe that I could ever be friends with him.

Two years later, I got an email from him asking for forgiveness. It was a nice email, but my instincts were to ask him what he wanted. He said he didn't want anything other than my forgiveness to alleviate his feelings of guilt.

We went back and forth on email for a while. At some point I asked him to come over and help me do something and he jumped at the chance.

From there forward, we've had a wonderful loving and supportive friendship. I would never have dreamed that my love for him could ever evolve into a deeper more honest, more kind, more loving relationship than I had ever had with him.

He is one of the most important people in my life. I know that I can call on him for anything which makes me feel safe in a weird world.

The next time an old love comes back into your life and you have an opportunity to forgive, consider it. It might be a great decision.

CAREER AND PURPOSE

62

stop listening to dream critics.

Most people want you to live a small life because it makes them feel safe. But your life goal is not to make your family and friends feel safe. Live big.

Your family and friends will be fine.

When I started my business I was told by a friend to be careful who I talked to about my goals. What I found was that there were folks who discouraged me from dreaming big because they didn't want me to struggle or be disappointed when it didn't work out. They were coming from a place of love. Unfortunately, these folks were in the minority.

Most people who discouraged me did so out of their own fear. Their negativity was a reflection of their own pain for choosing to live a smaller, safer life.

I backed away from many friendships. Now, while I have fewer people in my life, I'm surrounded by those who support my big dreams because they have big dreams too.

The next time someone discourages you, ask yourself if they are coming from a place of love or fear.

63

live an alternative life.

I sold juice and soda in a strip club to support myself while in therapy. It was a great job, and one of my best life experiences. It taught me that there are lots of ways to make money outside of Corporate America. Money is green and it doesn't matter how you make it.

That experience made moving in and out of Corporate America much easier. Many are programmed to only consider 9-5 positions that offer healthcare and paid vacations. I suspect they are afraid of what would happen if they were the CEO of their life.

If you have the chance to live an alternative life, do it. You'll be better for it, and probably much happier.

64

change your relationship to money.

We have serious limiting beliefs around making lots of money. Many think that you have to take advantage of someone to get rich. Or, good people don't get rich because they are honest.

The truth is that money can be made in a variety of ways. It can also be spent in a variety of ways. We get to choose.

If you are struggling with making money or keeping money, you probably have self-limiting beliefs around money. The good news is that you can change those beliefs.

Remember, we have complete control over our feelings and beliefs so choose wisely.

65

redefine success.

Having a lot of money is nice but I want freedom. Freedom to stay in bed when I'm sick. Take a nap in a hammock when I'm tired. Go sailing if I don't have any pressing work. Having the freedom to do as I please doesn't take a lot of money, but it does make me feel rich.

Think about what your life would be like if you have a lot of money. What would that money afford you to do? Then ask yourself if money was really required to enjoy that activity. Sometimes, it's not.

66

follow the fear.

Growth, change, and transformation: they don't happen when you're comfortable. Follow your fear because that is where you will find fulfillment.

When I do something right, I don't learn from the experience, which is not so bad. But if I only do what I know, life becomes small real fast.

Step out of your comfort zone if you want a bigger, more fulfilling life. It's the only way to learn new skills that will expand your life.

Follow the fear.

67

reinvent yourself.

If who you were yesterday, last month, or last year no longer feels authentic, release it to the universe. It no longer serves you so there is no need to hold on to it. In fact, it will hold you back.

This is my work history: market researcher, cocktail waitress in a strip club, fine art painter, temp receptionist, textile designer, corporate communications person, director of business development for a consulting firm, appointment setter, owner of a woodturning business, Etsy seller, cold calling coach, owner of sales consulting firm, Airbnb host, empathic intuitive healer, author, and speaker.

This is not a career path. It's called following your dreams.

If you are someone who can work at a job you don't like, God bless. There is nothing wrong with that.

If you are someone who needs to love what they do for a living, God bless. There is also nothing wrong with that.

68

stop comparing yourself to others.

We are all on our own journeys. Everyone has obstacles to overcome. Don't covet someone's journey. You can't have it and that is okay.

I do this all the time because I feel like I'm behind or that I'm a late bloomer. It's really easy to be peaceful when you live at the top of a mountain alone. It's so much harder when you live among people.

Whenever I see someone succeed at something that I want for myself, I think "Good for them. They deserve it. My turn is coming up." It helps me stay grateful.

You have your own path to blaze. Stay on it.

69

be you.

The World doesn't have room for another _____ , but it does have room for you if you stay true to yourself.

This is so true if you are an artist. There is always room for new ideas. But there isn't room for someone who paints exactly like Matisse.

Find your style, a style that no one can claim as their own. There will be room for you. I promise.

70

declare that you are an artist, writer, painter, woodturner, etc.

This is really hard for those of us who are self-taught.

At what point are you an artist? Is it 10,000 hours of experience, a diploma, the ability to support yourself, or a gallery show?

You have permission to call yourself an artist right now.

01:01*Give yourself permission to . . .*

71

believe that you can do anything.

I know to my core that I can handle anything that comes my way. Some obstacles might take longer to overcome but I will always land on my feet in a better place. Knowing this has allowed me to take bigger risks because I am not afraid of making mistakes. I'll always be okay.

This took me decades to learn. I think I was in my mid-forties when my fear subsided. Before that, I had panic attacks over things that might happen in a month.

Please don't put yourself through the anxiety that I put myself through. You have lots of options. If you calm down, you'll see the opportunities and maybe even get excited about some of them.

72

quit your job.

I'm someone who needs to love their work. I can't work for a company I don't believe in, a boss who I don't respect, and coworkers who I don't enjoy. As an empath, not being in total alignment sucks the life out of me.

I was so miserable at one job that I left at the end of the day and never came back. It felt great to simply walk away.

We spend the majority of our waking hours at work. A great job gives you a sense of purpose, feeds your soul, helps you grow personally and professionally, and more.

If your current job doesn't enhance your life in any way, give yourself permission to quit your job.

73

wait for the dust to settle
before making a decision.

I'm really impulsive and I can convince myself of almost anything. Knowing this, I'm really careful when I have to make a decision. If I'm feeling a sense of urgency, I know it's coming from an old wound. I wait until the dust settles before I commit.

One night I had this great idea about giving someone my undivided attention. I thought I could create a business based on listening to people. I would become a professional listener. Tada! (Eye roll)

I convinced myself to move to Los Angeles because folks there are early adopters of woo-woo things. In the morning I even called someone about building a website. (Eye roll)

I put everything else in my life on hold to pursue this idea.

Once the dust settled I realized that, while an interesting idea, it probably wasn't the smartest idea.

The next time you feel a sense of urgency to do something, slow down and wait for the dust to settle before you invest a lot of time and energy.

74

make a career change.

I've made more pivots in my life than a ballerina. I have had probably seven or eight different careers. I went to five colleges. I change boyfriends every four years. For some reason, I evolve really quickly and find myself in a completely different place than I was a year or two ago.

If you're like me, people may advise you to stick to one thing, which to me screams boredom.

I need to be in love with what I do for a living. I was a woodturner and worked at home in my woodshop. After ten years I realized that there was something more lucrative and safer. The thought of being alone in the woods with a chainsaw at sixty-five years old was too risky. I can't see a reason why I should have stayed committed to woodturning.

If you're like me, I think we have really interesting lives. We are great dinner party guests. People consider us fascinating and brave.

75

ask for a raise.

Long gone are the days where loyalty and hard work are financially rewarded. If you want a raise, you have to ask for it.

The first year I was a salesperson I didn't make much money because I had no experience. I was fine with that. The second year, however, I knew that I was worth a lot more.

I created a presentation that included all the new business I was responsible for bringing in. Honestly, it wasn't much, but then I added all the relationships I had created. That list was impressive.

I met with the owner and reviewed the presentation. He agreed that I did deserve a raise, but he couldn't give it to me at the moment. When the end of the year came, I got a big bonus and significant raise.

Had I not asked, I'm sure I would have been given an increase, but I doubt I would have been given as much.

Yes, it is uncomfortable to ask for a raise, but it's also normal. People ask for raises every day and survive. Go for it!

76

reject advice.

Not every piece of advice is directed to you. Sometimes the advice comes from someone who needs to hear it themselves.

I've been given terrible advice over the years. A psychiatrist told me once that I was too old to make a career change and that I need to "just pick one thing you can make money doing and do it."

When someone offers unsolicited advice, simply reject the advice with as much grace as possible.

77

stop panicking about money.

If you concentrate on not having enough money, you will live a life of not having enough money.

Another way to say it: You get what you worry about.

Another way to say it: You get what you think about.

This is a struggle for me because I have huge money issues. I try very hard to correct my thoughts when I panic about money.

Instead of worrying where it will come from, I tell myself things like: I'm really looking forward to receiving a boatload of cash this week; or I'm excited to be finally out of debt.

Remember, control your thoughts or they will control you!

78

want to be rich and famous.

I want to be rich and famous. I admit it.

I have my own reasons, some of which are based on my need to gain approval from people who I perceive to be more successful than I.

I'd like to live in luxury. I don't know what that is like but I'd like to try it.

I'd also like to have complete financial serenity.

I'd also like the opportunity to experience the disappointment that being rich and famous doesn't make you happy.

Becoming rich and famous is a double edge sword. I welcome the good and bad. It's a wild ride that I'd love to experience, and it's okay that you do too.

79

redefine success.

Success to me is freedom.

I want to be able to stay in bed to take care of my migraine or stack wood during the day and work at night. I want to take a nap when I need one.

Give yourself permission to use something other than money to define success.

80

need to love how you make money.

I'm not motivated by money. I'm motivated by helping people. It's what I love and what I'm good at.

I could never work just for the money because it would mean that I'm working to save money to enjoy at a later date. I need to be happy today, not this weekend or when it's time to go on vacation or when I retire.

It's okay to need to love how you earn a living.

FAMILY

81

love a person's soul but
not their physical
manifestation in this lifetime.

In this lifetime, it may be impossible to love someone and that's okay.

I don't like my biological family and am fine that they are not in my life. I'll reconnect with them in the afterlife.

If you find yourself in a position where you have to remove someone from your life, realize that you can still love their soul.

82

divorce your family.

If you can divorce the parent of your children, you can certainly divorce your family. It need not be a big declaration. It can be as simple as saying to yourself that you no longer want to be a part of that family.

After years of no contact, I said to myself that I no longer wanted to be a Younge. I changed my name to Standish, which surprisingly freed me from my past. It was the right choice for me. It might be the right choice for you too.

Think long and hard. Divorcing your family may be just what you need to move forward.

83

think your parents are bananas.

My mother's tongue is as sharp as a snake. She could be incredibly cruel. She never apologized because her rule was that if she said something that hurt my feelings, that it's my job to forgive her. WHAT?!?!?!

That is bananas. Who in the world thinks this way? Unbelievable.

My parents had children very young because my mother felt the pressure to have kids even though she didn't want them. (She told us.)

I don't give them a pass. They were adults and should have made better decisions. I love their souls. Their souls are loving, kind, supportive, understanding, nourishing, and fun. In their physical manifestation, not so much.

If you struggle with loving someone you don't want in your life, consider loving their soul.

84

not read minds.

Unless you are a psychic, it is unreasonable for your partner to expect that you should know what they are thinking. The hallmark of a successful relationship is effective communication.

My mother expected us as children to read her mind especially when it came to gifts. She believed that if we loved her, we would know what gift to buy her.

The PRESSURE.

Demand clear communication in every aspect of your life. It establishes boundaries and expectations, reduces mistakes and hurt feelings, and makes people feel as if they have been heard.

Loving someone doesn't mean you know what they are thinking.

If someone says, "If you loved me you would know _____ ," run for the hills.

85

wake someone up.

The number one rule in my childhood home was don't wake Mom. Actually, the number one rule was be skinny or no one will love you.

The second rule was don't wake Mom. If you did, she would come flying down the stairs screaming at you. We were all afraid of her, even my father.

Read the permission about flushing the toilet at night for more information.

If you have a good reason to wake someone up, do it.

86

be angry that you have
to parent yourself.

When I was around ten years old, I was left at a grocery store. My mother said she saw me get in the car but, I didn't get in the car. I went to put the cart away. When I turned around, I saw her and my two sisters driving away, onto the highway, and then gone.

I chased after them sobbing, "Wait for me. Wait for me."

At some point, one of my sisters asked my mother why she left me at the grocery store.

Eventually, they returned. I jumped in the back seat.

My mother probably said something like, "I thought I saw you get in the back seat."

But there was no apology. She never hugged me and told me that she would never leave me anywhere. Or that she panicked as soon as she realized what had happened and raced back to the store to get me.

I got nothing.

I had to put myself back together.

You don't need permission to be angry that you had to parent yourself when you were a child.

Get angry but don't stay angry. Forgive so that you can move on. Forgiveness doesn't mean you open the door to let them return.

87

not celebrate Christmas.

My mother measured how much people loved her by the gifts they gave her. Not surprisingly, this put a lot of pressure on me as a child to find the perfect gift.

The first Christmas after I graduated college I asked everyone in the family if we could skip presents this year because I had no discretionary income.

The fallout was extreme. My mother cried. Everyone else was in shock. I had ruined Christmas all because I had no extra money to buy people gifts.

I never celebrated Christmas again and I'm happier for it. I get to enjoy time off when everyone else is shopping frantically, spending money they don't have on gifts for people who they probably don't like much.

I prefer to give "I love you" gifts throughout the year. If I see something that I know someone would like, I buy it and give it to them. Simple. No pressure. I get the pleasure of surprising someone with a gift and the recipient gets the pleasure of receiving a surprise gift.

Please don't let society force you into celebrating a holiday if you don't want to. Lots of people don't celebrate Christmas and they do just fine.

88

hold enablers accountable.

While my mother was outwardly the most abusive, my father played a huge part in the abuse because he did nothing.

He could have intervened. He could have protected us. He could have done a lot of things, but he didn't.

Don't give enablers a pass. They don't deserve it.

89

believe that your version of
events as a child are just as valid
as an adult's version.

If you were to ask my mother if she ran around the house like a crazy person she would say no. But from my point of view as a child, she did run around the house like a crazy person.

Who is right? Both of us are.

Your version of events as a child are just as valid as an adult's. Don't let anyone talk you out of it.

90

flush the toilet at night.

When I was six years old, I went to the bathroom and flushed the toilet when I was finished. I, in my little yellow pajamas with a duck on the front, froze. I could not move. I knew what was coming for me.

My mother rushed into the bathroom, arms waving in the air screaming, "How could you? How could you? You woke me up."

I woke up a stay-at-home mother who was allowed to sleep until 10 a.m. every day of her life. Because she was so terrible in the mornings, my father had to get three grade-school girls ready for the bus every day.

How could being woken up in the middle of the night by a toilet flushing trigger such a hostile response? I will never know.

Please flush the toilet at night. For me. Flush as many times as you want.

ONE LAST THOUGHT ...

91

enjoy the moment.

As an overachiever, I'm always looking forward to the next thing. But life doesn't happen in the future. It happens now … . And now … . And now.

It's important to sit still and enjoy this moment in time. You only get to enjoy today, for one day.

About the Author

JENNIFER STANDISH *is a transformational coach and an intuitive healer certified by the Institute of Intuitive Healing.*

In her early 20s, Jennifer's mentor told her that if she stayed on the "corporate highway", she would retire with a perfect resume, but if she got off the highway and on to the backroads, she would have an amazing life and retire with great stories. She wanted the amazing life.

Once on the backroads, Jennifer enjoyed life as a fine art primitive painter, textile designer, and owner of Rooster Studios, a woodturning studio that sold a line of kitchenware worldwide.

To occasionally make ends meet, Jennifer went back to Corporate America, where she learned how to cold call, a skill that eventually became Prospecting Works, a cold calling consulting firm. Her work with people who had severe call reluctance led her to transformational coaching.

"Supporting people as they conquer low self-esteem, self-limiting beliefs, impostor syndrome, severe anxiety, and career crises is a privilege. I hope to spend the rest of my days bringing people out of the dark and into the light," she says.

Jennifer lives in Los Angeles, CA, where she has an active private practice. When not seeing clients, hosting workshops, or speaking, she is learning how to sail.

For more great books from Mythic Literary Press

Visit Books.GracePointPublishing.com

If you enjoyed reading *Permission Granted: Live Your Life Full of Joy and Peace,*
and purchased it through an online retailer,
please return to the site and write a review to help others find the book.

www.ingramcontent.com/pod-product-compliance
Lightning Source LLC
Chambersburg PA
CBHW060049100426
42742CB00014B/2747